# Using a Dictionary

## BY
## DEBORAH WHITE BROADWATER

COPYRIGHT © 2001 Mark Twain Media, Inc.

ISBN 1-58037-162-0

Printing No. CD-1383

Mark Twain Media, Inc., Publishers
Distributed by Carson-Dellosa Publishing Company, Inc.

# Table of Contents

**DICTIONARY**

# Table of Contents

DICTIONARY

# Using a Dictionary: *Introduction*

A **dictionary** is a book used to look up the spelling and meaning of words. A dictionary is also used to help you find the pronunciation of a word and whether or not it should be capitalized. In a dictionary there is information about how many syllables are in a word, what part of speech a word is, and what the synonyms and antonyms are for a word. Dictionaries may also tell the history of a word and when it is appropriate to use it.

Some dictionaries present this information in different ways, but there are general features in all dictionaries. Students should read the introductory section in the dictionaries they will use. This will help them to better use their dictionaries.

Below is a general pronunciation key that may be copied and given to students as a reference. The introductory page of each section also contains useful reference information that should be copied and given to students before they complete the exercises.

This book explains how information is presented in a dictionary. Activities help students become familiar with the arrangement of a dictionary and how they can find the information they are seeking.

## Pronunciation Key

| | | | | |
|---|---|---|---|---|
| a | cap, bad | oi | oil, toy |
| ā | cane, age, save | ô | law, caught, off |
| ä | father, mark, ah | o͞o | tool, ooze, moo |
| e | met, end, said | o͝o | wool, book, put, should |
| ē | be, equal, piece, key | ou | house, out, now |
| ər | baker, maker | sh | she, dash, machine |
| ə | ago, complete, taken, pencil, circus | th | thin, both |
| hw | white, whether, which | *th* | this, mother, smooth |
| i | pit, in | u | up, mud, love, double |
| ī | ice, fine, my | ū | use, mule, cue, feud, few |
| îr | ear, deer, here, pierce | ü | rule, true, food |
| o | pop, odd | ür | burn, hurry, term, bird, word |
| ō | hold, toe | | |

# Alphabetical Order: *Introduction*

All dictionaries are arranged in alphabetical order. It is important to know the alphabet, because the words in a dictionary are alphabetized by each letter. For example, a word with the first letter, "a," comes before words with all other first letters. Also, a word with the second letter "a," comes before words with second letters after "a." *Animal* comes before *buffalo*, but *animal* also comes before *animate* and on through all the letters of the word.

Abbreviations are usually in the main part of a dictionary. However, some dictionaries have a special section for them. Abbreviations are alphabetized by the abbreviation and not by the word they stand for. *Blvd.* for *Boulevard* will be found after *blind* and before *bone.* The exception to this is *st.* for *saint*, which will be with the word *saint.* For example, *St. Louis* will be completely spelled out as *Saint Louis.*

Name: _____  Date: _____

# Alphabetical Order: *Exercise 1*  DICTIONARY

**Directions:** Write each list in alphabetical order on the line below each set of words.

1.  nut        salute      paint       north       bitter

    _____

2.  map        noon        beach       ocean       mast

    _____

3.  breathe    salon       cobra       collision   auto

    _____

4.  numb       dive        mummy       bluff       animal

    _____

5.  gentle     quick       puppy       beauty      wave

    _____

6.  pickle     doughnut    candy       spaghetti   window

    _____

7.  salt       cartoon     lucky       onion       kangaroo

    _____

8.  answer     question    balloon     many        lucky

    _____

9.  wishful    donkey      zero        wonderful   enough

    _____

10. hungry     eating      sandwich    juice       hot dog

    _____

Name: _____ Date: _____

# Alphabetical Order: *Exercise 2* DICTIONARY

**Directions:** Write each list in alphabetical order on the line below each set of words.

1. middle   marker   mean   money   mast   mince   mouse   milk   mildew

   _____

2. answer   amber   announce   awake   applaud   amble   aisle   ajar   acorn

   _____

3. dinner   door   dance   dapple   dangle   drop   drive   dunce   deny

   _____

4. posture   plea   path   prize   pride   plow   paid   phone   purse

   _____

5. bitter   bluff   bicycle   back   bake   bend   blink   buffalo   botch

   _____

6. throw   think   tank   trim   tailor   torn   table   teller   tick

   _____

7. name   neon   noon   nape   north   numb   nose   nine   nothing

   _____

8. sassy   saber   sister   settle   simple   south   scissors   skeleton   sample

   _____

9. cobra   came   color   candle   come   collision   combat   cider   center

   _____

10. quiz   quit   quilt   quiet   quell   quaint   quite   quizzical   quince

   _____

Name: _____ Date: _____

# Alphabetical Order: *Exercise 3* DICTIONARY

**Directions:** Arrange the following words and abbreviations in alphabetical order.

wandering          1. _____

marvelous          2. _____

divine             3. _____

curtail            4. _____

statesman          5. _____

money              6. _____

Rd.                7. _____

Dept.              8. _____

question           9. _____

minute            10. _____

water lily        11. _____

suppose           12. _____

muddle            13. _____

Prof.             14. _____

discriminate      15. _____

confuse           16. _____

department store  17. _____

anniversary       18. _____

elephant          19. _____

human being       20. _____

# Alphabetical Order: *Exercise 4* DICTIONARY

**Directions:** Arrange the following words and abbreviations in alphabetical order.

deep          1. _____

depend        2. _____

dance         3. _____

direct        4. _____

distant       5. _____

dream         6. _____

deport        7. _____

defense       8. _____

doughnut      9. _____

dear          10. _____

dip           11. _____

Dr.           12. _____

drove         13. _____

dept.         14. _____

dent          15. _____

drift         16. _____

danger        17. _____

dye           18. _____

die           19. _____

donut         20. _____

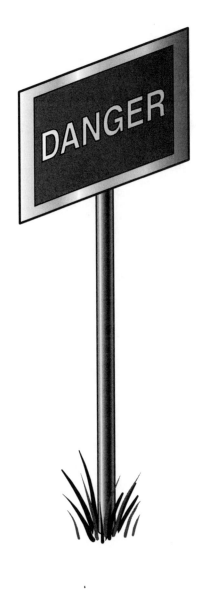

Name: _____ Date: _____

# Alphabetical Order: *Exercise 5* DICTIONARY

**Directions:** Arrange the following words and abbreviations in alphabetical order.

honor          1. _____

home           2. _____

host           3. _____

hope           4. _____

hold           5. _____

hobby          6. _____

hopper         7. _____

homogenize     8. _____

honorary       9. _____

holder         10. _____

home base      11. _____

horizontal     12. _____

Holocaust      13. _____

how            14. _____

homing         15. _____

horse          16. _____

hoot           17. _____

hog-tie        18. _____

hockey         19. _____

hour           20. _____

# Word Placement: *Introduction*

All dictionaries are arranged in alphabetical order. A dictionary can be divided into three parts with A, B, C, D, and E in the first third; F, G, H, I, J, K, L, M, N, O, and P in the middle third; and Q, R, S, T, U, V, W, X, Y, and Z in the last third. If you think of a dictionary in this way, it will make it easier and faster to find the word you are searching for.

For example, if you are looking for the word *candle*, you know that it will be in the first third of the dictionary; the word *pizza* will be in the middle third; and the word *tulip* will be in the last third.

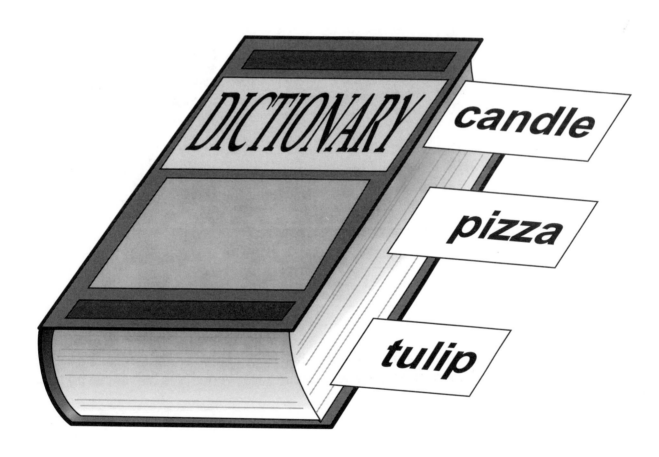

Name: _____ Date: _____

# Word Placement: *Exercise 1* DICTIONARY

**Directions:** Decide if these words would come in the **first** third, the **middle** third, or the **last** third of the dictionary.

nonsense            1. _____

underhanded       2. _____

pickle                 3. _____

animal                4. _____

welcome             5. _____

silence                6. _____

lemon                 7. _____

young                 8. _____

rascal                 9. _____

current              10. _____

velum                11. _____

quiet                 12. _____

inch                  13. _____

manual              14. _____

bamboo             15. _____

Practice dictionary placement with a partner. Have him or her say a word, then you try to open the dictionary to the correct third. Next, tell your partner a word and have him or her try to open the dictionary to the correct third.

Name: _____  Date: _____

# Word Placement: *Exercise 2* DICTIONARY

**Directions:** Decide if these words would come in the **first** third, the **middle** third, or the **last** third of the dictionary.

lullaby           1. _____

apricot           2. _____

stable            3. _____

minnow            4. _____

quickly           5. _____

wonderful         6. _____

honest            7. _____

enormous          8. _____

persuade          9. _____

leprechaun        10. _____

oyster            11. _____

routine           12. _____

bashful           13. _____

juniper           14. _____

turmoil           15. _____

Practice dictionary placement with a partner. Have him or her say a word, then you try to open the dictionary to the correct third. Next, tell your partner a word and have him or her try to open the dictionary to the correct third.

Name: _____ Date: _____

# Word Placement: *Exercise 3* DICTIONARY

**Directions:** A dictionary is divided into thirds, **A–E, F–P,** and **Q–Z.** Decide which letters these words would come between in the dictionary. Write those letters on the line below each word.

1. garage

_____

2. buffalo

_____

3. manly

_____

4. strain

_____

5. prune

_____

6. jump

_____

7. winter

_____

8. decide

_____

9. igloo

_____

10. umbrella

_____

11. runner

_____

12. note

_____

13. cracker

_____

14. obscure

_____

15. yank

_____

16. wheat

_____

17. prickle

_____

18. triumph

_____

19. sputter

_____

20. wallpaper

_____

21. latitude

_____

22. rugby

_____

23. benefit

_____

24. fortify

_____

25. meander

_____

Name: _____  Date: _____

# Word Placement: *Exercise 4*  DICTIONARY

**Directions:** A dictionary is divided into thirds, **A–E, F–P,** and **Q–Z.** Decide which letters these words would come between in the dictionary. Write those letters on the line below each word.

1. paper

_____

2. actress

_____

3. jealous

_____

4. review

_____

5. assessment

_____

6. tractor

_____

7. mouse

_____

8. dictionary

_____

9. earphones

_____

10. booklet

_____

11. pitcher

_____

12. stereo

_____

13. candy

_____

14. streetcar

_____

15. gigantic

_____

16. watermelon

_____

17. cantaloupe

_____

18. banana

_____

19. freckle

_____

20. laughter

_____

21. microscope

_____

22. yellow

_____

23. boxer

_____

24. random

_____

25. geyser

_____

Name: _____ Date: _____

# Word Placement: *Exercise 5*

Read each of the following words. Think about which section in your dictionary you would find that word. Try to open your dictionary to the correct place. What were the guide words on the page you turned to? Is your word on that page? What are the guide words for the word? Write the answers in the correct column.

| Word | Guide Words | Right Place? | Correct Guide Words |
|------|-------------|--------------|---------------------|
| 1. instant | _____ | _____ | _____ |
| 2. wonder | _____ | _____ | _____ |
| 3. bumper | _____ | _____ | _____ |
| 4. monster | _____ | _____ | _____ |
| 5. famous | _____ | _____ | _____ |
| 6. table | _____ | _____ | _____ |
| 7. computer | _____ | _____ | _____ |
| 8. kitchen | _____ | _____ | _____ |
| 9. enough | _____ | _____ | _____ |
| 10. justice | _____ | _____ | _____ |
| 11. violin | _____ | _____ | _____ |
| 12. dictionary | _____ | _____ | _____ |
| 13. open | _____ | _____ | _____ |
| 14. hopper | _____ | _____ | _____ |
| 15. blank | _____ | _____ | _____ |
| 16. discover | _____ | _____ | _____ |
| 17. incredible | _____ | _____ | _____ |
| 18. dubious | _____ | _____ | _____ |
| 19. hyphen | _____ | _____ | _____ |
| 20. photocopy | _____ | _____ | _____ |

# Guide Words: *Introduction* DICTIONARY

**Guide words** - Words in dictionaries are arranged in alphabetical order. At the top of each page are two guide words to help you find your word's page. These are the first and last words on that page. The one on the left is the first word on the page, and the one on the right is the last word on the page. For example, if the page has **cool** and **cope** at the top of the page, all the words on that page are between those two words in alphabetical order. To find the word you want, first find the page with the two guide words at the top that have the same letters as the word you are looking for. Then look down the page to find your word. If the word you are looking for comes before the guide word on the left, you must turn some pages toward the front of the book; if the word comes after the guide word on the right, you must turn some pages to the back of the dictionary.

For example, if you are looking for the word *brake* and the guide words are **bend** and **bicycle**, you will need to turn the pages toward the back of the dictionary because *bicycle*, the right guide word, comes before *brake*.

# Guide Words: *Exercise 1*  DICTIONARY

**Directions:** Look at the guide words and decide which words from the list will be on the dictionary page. Circle your answers.

1.  apple / balloon

    a. answer      b. arch        c. baboon

    d. angle       e. babble      f. bark

2.  dance / elephant

    a. elegant     b. danger      c. emperor

    d. dad         e. dive        f. each

3.  letter / mulch

    a. laugh       b. milk        c. lunch

    d. music       e. march       f. litter

4.  paid / quite

    a. pal         b. quiet       c. pill

    d. pay         e. padlock     f. quote

5.  mince / new

    a. money       b. name        c. now

    d. mare        e. multiply    f. never

6.  still / time

    a. talk        b. stay        c. stole

    d. tomb        e. tickle      f. stove

7.  postman / pothole

    a. potato      b. pound       c. pride

    d. posture     e. picnic      f. potent

Name: _____ Date: _____

# Guide Words: Exercise 2 DICTIONARY

**Directions:** Look at the guide words and decide which words from the list will be on the dictionary page. Circle your answers.

1. grant / grass

   a. grasp        b. grape        c. guilty

   d. grave        e. graph        f. grain

2. less / lever

   a. letter       b. lasso        c. level

   d. let          e. lettuce      f. limp

3. culture / cure

   a. crock        b. cupboard     c. curd

   d. curb         e. curtail      f. curfew

4. air / albatross

   a. ajar         b. Alaska       c. apple

   d. alarm        e. adjective    f. airport

5. hero / hiccup

   a. hibernate    b. handle       c. hello

   d. hint         e. hesitate     f. hew

6. painter / pest

   a. pad          b. patient      c. ponder

   d. peddle       e. pace         f. peace

7. uncap / uncross

   a. ultimate     b. uncle        c. uncork

   d. unchain      e. under        f. uncut

Name: _____ Date: _____

# Guide Words: *Exercise 3* DICTIONARY

**Directions:** Look at the guide words and decide which words from the list will be on the dictionary page. Circle your answers.

1. opportunity / organ

   a. orbit           b. oppose          c. operation

   d. ornament        e. orange          f. orderly

2. corduroy / corrupt

   a. coping          b. corn            c. correct

   d. corrosive       e. cosmic          f. cornice

3. shaft / shave

   a. shaker          b. shall           c. shade

   d. sharp           e. shawl           f. shame

4. melody / merge

   a. meter           b. menial          c. mercy

   d. melting         e. mend            f. meek

5. always / amnesia

   a. amend           b. ambush          c. alike

   d. amble           e. among           f. amuse

6. feature / fell

   a. feel            b. feeder          c. federal

   d. female          e. feeble          f. fern

7. relish / remove

   a. remark          b. relief          c. remember

   d. render          e. relapse         f. relive

16

Name: _____ Date: _____

# Guide Words: *Exercise 4* DICTIONARY

**Directions:** Look at the guide words and decide which words from the list will be on the dictionary page. Circle your answers.

1. residue / restless

   a. retina        b. rest        c. resistant      d. responsive

   e. resort        f. repulsion   g. resident       h. respect

2. grant / grease

   a. gray          b. grey        c. grave          d. granule

   e. gravel        f. graphite    g. gratuity       h. granite

3. calendar / camp

   a. calf          b. camera      c. camshaft       d. California

   e. calculus      f. cake        g. call           h. caulk

4. overripe / own

   a. oversleep     b. overrate    c. oxbow          d. overt

   e. owlet         f. overstep    g. ownership      h. override

5. crisp / crouch

   a. crossfire     b. crow        c. croak          d. crony

   e. critic        f. croquet     g. croup          h. crop

6. allow / also

   a. alternate     b. already     c. altar          d. allocate

   e. alloy         f. almanac     g. almond         h. allspice

7. lather / law

   a. laser         b. laugh       c. lava           d. leaden

   e. laundry       f. lattice     g. latrine        h. larva

Name: _____ Date: _____

# Guide Words: *Exercise 5* DICTIONARY

**Directions:** Look at the guide words listed at the left and decide if the word in the middle column will be **on** the dictionary page, **before** the dictionary page, or **after** the dictionary page indicated by those guide words.

1.  famous / foster          football          _____

2.  bead / beautiful        baker             _____

3.  tooth / top              touch             _____

4.  amble / animal          armor             _____

5.  caught / cedar          cease             _____

6.  deflate / degree        delay             _____

7.  mitt / mole              mistake           _____

8.  correct / corsage      correspond        _____

9.  rat / rattler            rash              _____

10. explore / express      extinct           _____

11. shadow / shallow       shanty            _____

12. dive / division        diversion         _____

13. scribble / scrub        scuba             _____

14. aspire / assume        aspic             _____

15. teepee / tennis        terminal          _____

16. graduation / grammar   grandmother       _____

17. lame / language        laminate          _____

18. round / rubbery        rouge             _____

19. midriff / milkman      millennium        _____

20. horsefly / hound       hostess           _____

# Guide Words: *Exercise 6* DICTIONARY

**Directions:** Look at the guide words listed at the left and decide if the word in the middle column will be **on** the dictionary page, **before** the dictionary page, or **after** the dictionary page indicated by those guide words.

1. deceit / decipher     decision     _____

2. oral / order     orange     _____

3. enforce / English     enhance     _____

4. underground / understand     undercut     _____

5. park / parted     parole     _____

6. granulate / grating     gravity     _____

7. radio / ragweed     radon     _____

8. multiply / muscle     municipal     _____

9. fund / fuselage     fur     _____

10. hind / hippo     himself     _____

11. vase / veil     velocity     _____

12. inactive / incense     impure     _____

13. necktie / neglect     neither     _____

14. jail / January     janitor     _____

15. zap / zero     zest     _____

16. safeguard / salesman     sailboat     _____

17. conquer / consist     connive     _____

18. anchovy / anger     anemia     _____

19. waist / wallet     waitress     _____

20. jiggle / joggle     jostle     _____

# Meaning: *Introduction* DICTIONARY

Each word listed is called a **main entry word.** These are the words that are listed in alphabetical order on the page. The main entry word will be spelled correctly, capitalized correctly, and divided into syllables. After the main entry word will be the part of speech. It will be an abbreviation for noun - **n**, verb - **v**, adjective - **adj**, adverb - **adv**, preposition - **prep**, or pronoun - **pron**.

The explanation of a word is called the **definition.** Sometimes words have one meaning; sometimes there are several. When there is more than one meaning, the definitions are numbered. Definitions are usually just a few words or phrases, rather than a complete sentence. When you are searching for just the right word for something you are writing, it is important to read all the definitions to make sure the word you choose will be the best choice.

It is important to know how the word is used in a sentence. If you know the word is used as an adjective, you will know that you don't need the definitions for the word as a noun or verb; they will not fit the context of your sentence.

Name: _____ Date: _____

# Meaning: *Exercise 1*  DICTIONARY

**Directions:** In each of the following sentences, decide which of the two meanings best fits the boldfaced word as it is used in the sentence. Write the letter on the blank space.

_____ 1. Due to a snowstorm, school was **dismissed** early.

   a. discharged from office or employment        b. to direct or allow to leave

_____ 2. We tested the **bark** to see how old the tree was.

   a. the sound made by a dog        b. the outer covering of a tree

_____ 3. Jane was feeling **blue** because she got a poor grade on her test.

   a. a color        b. gloomy or depressed

_____ 4. The **wind** is coming out of the east this morning.

   a. to wrap something around an object        b. moving air

_____ 5. Does your mother play the **organ** at school?

   a. a musical instrument        b. part of a human

_____ 6. I have the **lead** in the play this year.

   a. to show the way        b. the principal role

_____ 7. Our town is on the **bank** of the Mississippi River.

   a. the shore of a river        b. a place where money is kept

_____ 8. Carol knew she would like to have a **pickle** on her sandwich.

   a. a small preserved cucumber        b. an embarrassing or difficult situation

_____ 9. It is your **right** to choose which book you will read.

   a. that which is due by law or tradition        b. opposite of left

_____ 10. I can't **bear** the wait until my birthday comes.

   a. a large mammal        b. to endure

Name: _____ Date: _____

# Meaning: *Exercise 2*   DICTIONARY

**Directions:** In each of the following sentences, decide which of the two meanings best fits the boldfaced word as it is used in the sentence. Write the letter on the blank space.

_____ 1. Mrs. Lopez is very **fair** when she grades tests.

        a. not stormy weather      b. honest and just      c. not dark, but blond

_____ 2. If you follow this highway, it will **lead** you to a town.

        a. show the way      b. place in front      c. a metal

_____ 3. The old tree in the yard could **block** the noon sun from the porch.

        a. a piece of wood      b. keep from view      c. platform for selling

_____ 4. My mother belongs to a group that wants to **preserve** the forests.

        a. to prepare food      b. a type of jelly or jam      c. to keep for the future

_____ 5. The **panel** of judges watched the beauty contest.

        a. wood used for walls      b. a piece of material for sewing      c. a group of people

_____ 6. We have a **crack** in the ceiling of our basement.

        a. a small opening      b. a remark made by someone      c. a loud noise

**Directions:** In a dictionary look up the word **decoration**. Write a sentence for each of the definitions. Make sure you use the word correctly.

_____

_____

_____

_____

_____

_____

_____

_____

Name: _____   Date: _____

# Meaning: *Exercise 3*  DICTIONARY

**Directions:** Using a dictionary, look up the boldfaced word and write the definition that best fits the meaning of the sentence.

1. My dad is going to **panel** the family room walls.

   _____

2. Our car trip will **cover** 2,000 miles this summer.

   _____

3. John tried with all his **might** to lift the box of books, but it was too heavy.

   _____

4. I played a tennis **match** with Susan last Saturday.

   _____

5. Mrs. Mason had a **grave** look on her face as she told us our test scores.

   _____

6. Would you please pass the pickle **relish**?

   _____

7. Have you ever had a headache near your **temple**?

   _____

8. Jennifer got the **part** of the old woman in the school play.

   _____

9. The tall buildings in the city **block** the sun.

   _____

10. Free lemonade will **draw** a crowd for the puppet show.

   _____

Name: _____  Date: _____

# Meaning: *Exercise 4*  DICTIONARY

**Directions:** Using a dictionary, look up each boldfaced word and write the definition that best fits the meaning of the sentence on the lines below.

1. My sister and I are going **abroad** next summer.

   _____

2. Michael **leafed** through the magazine while he waited for the doctor.

   _____

3. Karen's grade in class **hinges** on how well she does on the next test.

   _____

4. What **method** shall we use when we do the science experiment?

   _____

5. You are not allowed to fish in a game **preserve**.

   _____

6. My mom and dad decided to raise my **allowance** this year.

   _____

7. A **spark** from an electrical cord started the fire in my neighbor's house.

   _____

8. There was a **blanket** of snow on the ground when we looked out the window.

   _____

9. You need to stir the **batter** for three minutes before pouring it into the cake pan.

   _____

10. Could I **trouble** you for some help with my homework?

   _____

Name: _____ Date: _____

# Meaning: *Exercise 5*  DICTIONARY

**Directions:** Try to determine the meaning of the boldfaced words in the following sentences, using the clues from the sentence. Write the definition in your own words on the first line, then write the definition from a dictionary on the second line.

1. Carol's **cue** to say her lines was when Brian slammed the door shut.

   _____

   _____

2. My father keeps all his favorite books in his **study**.

   _____

   _____

3. Where do you think we should put the **volume** of ancient poetry?

   _____

   _____

4. Could you **enlist** the help of your friends when it's time to move the television?

   _____

   _____

5. I bought a **chance** on the big teddy bear when I was at the fair.

   _____

   _____

6. Do you put a **dash** between the syllables when you divide a word at the end of a line?

   _____

   _____

Name: _____ Date: _____

# Meaning: *Exercise 6*     DICTIONARY

**Directions:** Try to determine the meaning of the boldfaced words in the following sentences, using the clues from the sentence. Write the definition in your own words on the first line, then write the definition from a dictionary on the second line.

1.  We made the **right** choice not to cross the street because the light said "Don't Walk."

    _____

    _____

2.  My brother's best event in track is the 100-yard **dash**.

    _____

    _____

3.  Would you please turn the **volume** down on the radio?

    _____

    _____

4.  The weatherman said it **might** snow six inches overnight.

    _____

    _____

5.  The archer lifted the **bow**, pulled the arrow back, and shot toward the target.

    _____

    _____

6.  What speaker is going to **address** our graduating class at the assembly?

    _____

    _____

Name: _____ Date: _____

# Syllables: *Introduction* DICTIONARY

A **syllable** is a word or part of a word that can be spoken as a sound without interruption. Each syllable has only one vowel sound. The word *break* has one syllable. The word *bottom-less* has three syllables. In a dictionary, main entry words are divided into syllables. Dividing a word into syllables helps you to know how to pronounce it, and how to divide it at the end of a line when writing a sentence.

fathom;
descend to or
based or groun
**bot·tom·less** (-li
unlimited, b
etc.

Name: _____ Date: _____

# Syllables: *Exercise 1* DICTIONARY

**Directions:** Say each word to yourself. On the line below each word, rewrite the word, dividing it into syllables. Use dots, dashes, or spaces to divide the syllables. Use a dictionary if you need help.

1. potato

   _____

2. amber

   _____

3. feather

   _____

4. method

   _____

5. rodent

   _____

6. puzzle

   _____

7. lucky

   _____

8. tooth

   _____

9. shark

   _____

10. mattress

    _____

11. great

    _____

12. desk

    _____

13. trouble

    _____

14. urgent

    _____

28

Name: _____ Date: _____

# Syllables: *Exercise 2*  DICTIONARY

**Directions:** Say each word to yourself. On the line below each word, rewrite the word, dividing it into syllables. Use dots, dashes, or spaces to divide the syllables. Use a dictionary if you need help.

1. extraordinary

   _____

2. wonderful

   _____

3. television

   _____

4. succeeded

   _____

5. forever

   _____

6. stolen

   _____

7. ethical

   _____

8. desired

   _____

9. affectionate

   _____

10. chat

    _____

11. preserve

    _____

12. dessert

    _____

13. shining

    _____

14. quickly

    _____

Name: _____ Date: _____

# Syllables: *Exercise 3* DICTIONARY

**Directions:** Say each word to yourself. On the line below each word, rewrite the word, dividing it into syllables. Use dots, dashes, or spaces to divide the syllables. Use a dictionary if you need help.

1. trustworthy

   _____

2. antagonist

   _____

3. unbelievable

   _____

4. marvelous

   _____

5. synthetic

   _____

6. butterscotch

   _____

7. blanket

   _____

8. memory

   _____

9. sometimes

   _____

10. methodical

    _____

11. additional

    _____

12. particularly

    _____

13. complete

    _____

14. metropolis

    _____

*Butterscotch*

Name: _____ Date: _____

# Syllables: *Exercise 4* DICTIONARY

**Directions:** Say each word to yourself. Rewrite each of the following words, marking where you would divide these words into sylllables.

1. unhappy     _____

2. picture     _____

3. friendly     _____

4. lookout     _____

5. damage     _____

6. keyboard     _____

7. decide     _____

8. wishful     _____

9. party     _____

10. riddle     _____

11. distant     _____

12. early     _____

13. fender     _____

14. pickle     _____

15. puppy     _____

16. grenade     _____

17. sizzle     _____

18. marvel     _____

19. himself     _____

20. employ     _____

Name: _____  Date: _____

# Syllables: *Exercise 5* DICTIONARY

**Directions:** Say each word to yourself. On the blank beside each word, write its number of syllables.

1. unusual _____

2. special _____

3. distant _____

4. elephant _____

5. definition _____

6. classroom _____

7. clothing _____

8. brought _____

9. dismiss _____

10. phrase _____

11. unfamiliar _____

12. wheat _____

13. example _____

14. look _____

15. packet _____

16. assurance _____

17. predicament _____

18. supernatural _____

19. collapse _____

20. spiraling _____

21. factors _____

22. condition _____

23. evaluate _____

24. distance _____

25. speculation _____

26. disgruntled _____

27. inarticulate _____

28. situations _____

29. instigate _____

30. report _____

# Pronunciation: *Introduction* DICTIONARY

The **pronunciation** of a word in the dictionary comes right after the main entry word. It is written in a pronunciation spelling. This is also sometimes referred to as the dictionary spelling. This tells you how to say or pronounce the word. These letters are usually explained in the front or back of a dictionary. Often a shorter listing is at the bottom of the dictionary page. The key will give you words that have the same sound as the symbol. You need to know what these symbols mean in order to know how the word is pronounced.

The dictionary spelling leaves out letters that are not pronounced.

> brake = brak     The silent "e" is not written.

The dictionary spelling also shows which syllable is accented. This lets you know which syllable to emphasize.

| | | |
|---|---|---|
| present - a gift | = | prez′ ənt |
| present - to introduce | = | pri zent′ |

Name: _____ Date: _____

# Pronunciation: *Exercise 1* DICTIONARY

**Directions:** Use a dictionary pronunciation key. Find a word that is an example of the pronunciation for each of the following symbols. Write the word on the line and pronounce it to yourself.

1. z    _____

2. oi    _____

3. b    _____

4. i    _____

5. a    _____

6. âr    _____

7. ch    _____

8. ə    _____

9. f    _____

10. v    _____

11. e    _____

12. th    _____

13. n    _____

14. zh    _____

15. d    _____

Name: _____ Date: _____

# Pronunciation: *Exercise 2* DICTIONARY

**Directions:** Use a dictionary pronunciation key. Find a word that is an example of the pronunciation for each of the following symbols. Write the word on the line and pronounce it to yourself.

1. ā _____

2. y _____

3. ō _____

4. p _____

5. ng _____

6. g _____

7. sh _____

8. o͞o _____

9. r _____

10. t _____

11. ər _____

12. o _____

13. m _____

14. hw _____

15. ou _____

b r

ā

ng

o͞o

t

sh

Name: _____ Date: _____

# Pronunciation: *Exercise 3* DICTIONARY

**Directions:** Use a dictionary pronunciation key. Find a word that is an example of the pronunciation for each of the following symbols. Write the word on the line and pronounce it to yourself.

1. *th*    _____

2. w    _____

3. ē    _____

4. ä    _____

5. ûr    _____

6. l    _____

7. ŏŏ    _____

8. u    _____

9. s    _____

10. h    _____

11. ī    _____

12. ô    _____

13. j    _____

14. ə    _____

15. k    _____

Name: _____ Date: _____

# Pronunciation: *Exercise 4* DICTIONARY

**Directions:** Use a dictionary to find the correct pronunciation of each word. Write the pronunciation (dictionary spelling) on the line under the word. Then say the word to yourself using the pronunciation guide.

1. enough

   _____

2. weight

   _____

3. bold

   _____

4. object

   _____

5. candle

   _____

6. steak

   _____

7. never

   _____

8. idea

   _____

9. completely

   _____

10. rough

    _____

11. quickly

    _____

12. mellow

    _____

13. reign

    _____

14. cope

    _____

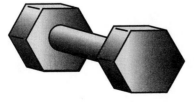 

Name: _____  Date: _____

# Pronunciation: *Exercise 5* DICTIONARY

**Directions:** Use a dictionary to find the correct pronunciation of each word. Write the pronunciation (dictionary spelling) on the line under the word. Then say the word to yourself using the pronunciation guide.

1. tension

   _____

2. defense

   _____

3. seize

   _____

4. roller

   _____

5. peaceful

   _____

6. observe

   _____

7. fearful

   _____

8. substitute

   _____

9. second

   _____

10. nation

    _____

11. poverty

    _____

12. immune

    _____

13. collection

    _____

14. slippery

    _____

Name: _____ Date: _____

# Pronunciation: *Exercise 6* DICTIONARY

**Directions:** Say each dictionary pronunciation below to yourself and choose the correct word from the word bank for each of the pronunciations.

| | | | | |
|---|---|---|---|---|
| overlay | fear | deaf | beach | pecan |
| carnival | roller | acre | horror | nose |
| catch | spat | television | speak | telephone |

1. pē kän′    _____

2. kär′ nə vəl    _____

3. fîr    _____

4. ā′ kər    _____

5. nōz    _____

6. kach    _____

7. spat    _____

8. rō′ lər    _____

9. def    _____

10. tel′ ə vizh′ ən    _____

11. spēk    _____

12. tel′ ə fōn′    _____

13. bēch    _____

14. hôr′ ər    _____

15. ō′ vər lā′    _____

Name: _____ Date: _____

# Pronunciation: *Exercise 7* DICTIONARY

**Directions:** Use the word bank to fill in the crossword puzzle. Use a dictionary if you need help.

| first | with | against | help | sometimes | every |
|-------|------|---------|------|-----------|-------|
| second | before | hurry | talk | weary | bottom |
| fourth | could | friend | stable | money | care |
| class | book | does | cake | creep | wish |
| rebate | | | | | |

| **ACROSS** | | |
|------------|--|--|
| 2. kood | 14. rē′ bāt′ | |
| 3. klas | 16. kâr | |
| 5. mun′ ē | 18. tôk | |
| 10. with | 19. duz | |
| 12. sum′ tīmz | 20. frend | |
| 13. bi fôr′ | 21. bot′ əm | |

| **DOWN** | |
|----------|--|
| 1. hûr′ ē | 9. wîr′ ē |
| 3. kāk | 11. fôrth |
| 4. stā′ bəl | 12. sek′ ənd |
| 6. ev′ rē | 15. ə genst′ |
| 7. fûrst | 16. krēp |
| 8. wish | 17. help |
| | 21. book |

40

Name: _____  Date: _____

# Pronunciation: *Exercise 8* DICTIONARY

**Directions:** Use the word bank to fill in the crossword puzzle. Use a dictionary if you need help.

| coed | bridge | remove | memory | month | tense |
|---|---|---|---|---|---|
| ebony | float | scarf | marine | delight | tubular |
| bison | ballot | affection | lagoon | drove | hallmark |
| general | bring | deceit | amid | hearty | charge |
| croak | | | | | |

### ACROSS
3. mə rēn′
6. ri moov′
8. lə goon′
10. chärj
11. kō′ ed′
13. too′ byə lər
14. flōt
17. eb′ ə nē
18. ə fek′ shən
20. di līt′
22. ə mid′
23. bring

### DOWN
1. brij
2. munth
3. mem′ ə rē
4. drōv
5. jen′ ə rəl
7. bal′ ət
9. scärf
12. bī′ sən
15. tens
16. hôl′ märk
19. krōk
20. di sēt′
21. här′ tē

# Prefixes and Suffixes: *Introduction*

A **prefix** is a syllable that is added to the beginning of a root word. Each prefix has a different meaning. Some examples of prefixes are: un-, dis-, non-, and pre-.

A **suffix** is an addition made at the end of a root word to change its meaning. Some examples of suffixes are: -ed, -ing, -ment, and -less.

Name: _____ Date: _____

# Prefixes and Suffixes: *Exercise 1* DICTIONARY

**Directions:** Add the prefix **un-**, **dis-**, **re-**, **non-**, or **pre-** to each of the words to form a new word. Write the new word on the line, underline the prefix you used, then write the definition of the new word. Use a dictionary if you need help.

1. living _____

_____

2. hurt _____

_____

3. agree _____

_____

4. do _____

_____

5. arrange _____

_____

6. working _____

_____

7. flammable _____

_____

8. soak _____

_____

9. lawful _____

_____

10. turn _____

_____

43

Name: _____ Date: _____

# Prefixes and Suffixes: *Exercise 2*

**Directions:** Add the prefix **un-**, **dis-**, **re-**, **non-**, or **pre-** to each of the words to form a new word. Write the new word on the line, underline the prefix you used, then write the definition of the new word. Use a dictionary if you need help.

1. stick _____

_____

2. usual _____

_____

3. appear _____

_____

4. cooperative _____

_____

5. refundable _____

_____

6. packaged _____

_____

7. dawn _____

_____

8. view _____

_____

9. happy _____

_____

10. stop _____

_____

Name: _____ Date: _____

# Prefixes and Suffixes: *Exercise 3*

**Directions:** Underline the suffix in each of the words below, then write the base word next to it. Using a dictionary, find the definition of the base word and write it on the line below.

1. beautiful   _____

   _____

2. dangerous   _____

   _____

3. breakable   _____

   _____

4. moving   _____

   _____

5. pitiful   _____

   _____

6. thoughtless   _____

   _____

7. drinkable   _____

   _____

8. strangest   _____

   _____

9. carrier   _____

   _____

10. reversible   _____

   _____

Name: _____ Date: _____

# Prefixes and Suffixes: *Exercise 4*

**Directions:** Underline the suffix in each of the words below, then write the base word next to it. Using a dictionary, find the definition of the base word and write it on the line below.

1. happiness    _____

   _____

2. wonderful    _____

   _____

3. laziest    _____

   _____

4. consumable    _____

   _____

5. foolish    _____

   _____

6. tiresome    _____

   _____

7. celebration    _____

   _____

8. employment    _____

   _____

9. persistence    _____

   _____

10. contentment    _____

   _____

Name: _____ Date: _____

# Prefixes and Suffixes: *Exercise 5*

**Directions:** For each of the following words, decide if the word has a prefix, a suffix, or both. Underline the prefix and/or circle the suffix and write the base word on the line.

1.  variable _____

2.  following _____

3.  disinterested _____

4.  sensible _____

5.  unhappily _____

6.  convertible _____

7.  disjointed _____

8.  reordered _____

9.  nonfiction _____

10. happiness _____

11. prearranged _____

12. unspeakable _____

13. nonpoisonous _____

14. misinformed _____

15. reconstruction _____

16. rightful _____

17. monotone _____

18. hydrotherapy _____

19. entanglement _____

20. uncomplicated _____

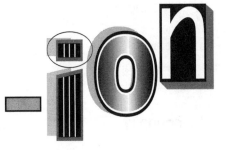

Name: _____  Date: _____

# Prefixes and Suffixes: *Exercise 6* DICTIONARY

**Directions:** For each of the following words, decide if the word has a prefix, a suffix, or both. Underline the prefix and/or circle the suffix and write the base word on the line.

1. defenseless        _____

2. runner             _____

3. excusable          _____

4. preschool          _____

5. wonderful          _____

6. friendliness       _____

7. nondairy           _____

8. unforgettable      _____

9. reusable           _____

10. miscast           _____

11. unanswerable      _____

12. willingness       _____

13. manageable        _____

14. succeeded         _____

15. disenchanted      _____

16. superhuman        _____

17. predestined       _____

18. exchange          _____

19. bimonthly         _____

20. quadraphonic      _____

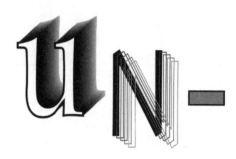

48

# Spelling: *Introduction* DICTIONARY

A dictionary can help you find the spelling of words. First, think about what the beginning sound of the word is. It can sometimes be misleading if the word begins with a letter that is silent, as in *knife* or *gnome.* However, for the most part, the sounds in the English language are often very helpful when looking up a word.

## Variant Spelling

Sometimes there is more than one spelling for a word; however, both spellings are correct.. The first spelling is the most commonly used; and the **variant** or alternate spelling follows.

## Plurals

The spelling of the **plural** form of the entry word is also listed. The plural is followed by **-pl**, meaning that it is the plural form. This is helpful to know when to change "y" to "i"; or to add "es"; or when to leave the "y" and just add "s." A dictionary will also show you what words are the same in the singular and plural forms, as in *deer*—singular and plural, not deers.

Name: _____ Date: _____

## Spelling: *Exercise 1* DICTIONARY

**Directions:** Look up each of the following words in a dictionary. If the word is spelled correctly, write **correct** on the blank. If it is not spelled correctly, write the correct spelling of the word on the blank.

1.  because        _____

2.  marter         _____

3.  separate       _____

4.  liscense       _____

5.  anser          _____

6.  underneath     _____

7.  calender       _____

8.  unhappy        _____

9.  spagetti       _____

10. rember         _____

11. accurrate      _____

12. swimmer        _____

13. frieght        _____

14. whisper        _____

15. fourty         _____

50

Name: _____ Date: _____

# Spelling: *Exercise 2*  DICTIONARY

**Directions:** Look up each of the following words in a dictionary. If the word is spelled correctly, write **correct** on the blank. If it is not spelled correctly, write the correct spelling of the word on the blank.

1. ache _____

2. suger _____

3. bouquay _____

4. condemn _____

5. offen _____

6. diffaculties _____

7. occurence _____

8. diseased _____

9. surprized _____

10. necessary _____

11. polacy _____

12. persuade _____

13. hatred _____

14. garantee _____

15. vaccuum _____

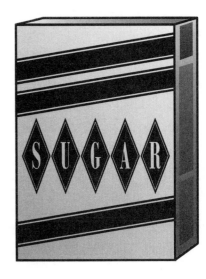

Name: _____ Date: _____

# Spelling: *Exercise 3*

# DICTIONARY

**Directions:** Look up each of the following words in a dictionary. If the word is spelled correctly, write **correct** on the blank. If it is not spelled correctly, write the correct spelling of the word on the blank.

1.  refe                    _____

2.  skeptic                _____

3.  experimental           _____

4.  nocternal              _____

5.  terrific               _____

6.  florol                 _____

7.  riting                 _____

8.  guide                  _____

9.  lesson                 _____

10. approvel               _____

11. buryal                 _____

12. crying                 _____

13. assinement             _____

14. swimming               _____

15. truely                 _____

Name: _____ Date: _____

# Spelling: *Exercise 4* DICTIONARY

**Directions:** Circle the word in each pair that is spelled correctly. Use a dictionary if you need help.

| | | | |
|---|---|---|---|
| 1. develope | develop | 16. argument | arguement |
| 2. worrisome | worrysome | 17. lovelyness | loveliness |
| 3. mistery | mystery | 18. meanness | meaness |
| 4. unusal | unusual | 19. advantageous | advantagous |
| 5. opportunity | oppertunity | 20. occured | occurred |
| 6. because | becuze | 21. beatiful | beautiful |
| 7. similer | similar | 22. jokeing | joking |
| 8. escape | excape | 23. believe | beleive |
| 9. operater | operator | 24. permiting | permitting |
| 10. adjourn | ajourn | 25. theif | thief |
| 11. alert | allert | 26. beged | begged |
| 12. neighbor | neigher | 27. tortoise | tortorse |
| 13. people | poeple | 28. receit | receipt |
| 14. autum | autumn | 29. priviledge | privilege |
| 15. tolerate | tolarate | 30. circular | circaler |

Name: _____ Date: _____

# Spelling: *Exercise 5*   DICTIONARY

**Directions:** Circle the word that is spelled correctly in each pair. Use a dictionary if you need help.

| | | | | |
|---|---|---|---|---|
| 1. happened | happend | 16. venum | venom |
| 2. craul | crawl | 17. nucaler | nuclear |
| 3. alirt | alert | 18. receive | recieve |
| 4. specal | special | 19. mooses | moose |
| 5. friend | freind | 20. different | diffrent |
| 6. illogical | ilogical | 21. compose | cumpose |
| 7. column | columm | 22. astronought | astronaut |
| 8. ansious | anxious | 23. monkies | monkeys |
| 9. yield | yeild | 24. expect | expekt |
| 10. elamentry | elementary | 25. scratch | scrach |
| 11. controlled | controled | 26. lanscape | landscape |
| 12. physian | physician | 27. recked | wrecked |
| 13. familer | familiar | 28. geese | gooses |
| 14. unecessary | unnecessary | 29. timming | timing |
| 15. conscience | consence | 30. vallies | valleys |

54

Name: _____ Date: _____

# Spelling: *Exercise 6 (Variant Spelling)* DICTIONARY

**Directions:** Using a dictionary, write the variant spelling for each of the following words. Put a star by the word that is used most often.

1.  canceled          _____

2.  cantaloupe        _____

3.  aesthetic         _____

4.  judgement         _____

5.  monolog           _____

6.  likeable          _____

7.  gage              _____

8.  harken            _____

9.  broach            _____

10. abridgement       _____

11. doughnut          _____

12. dialog            _____

13. cocoanut          _____

14. travelog          _____

15. rickshaw          _____

16. labor             _____

17. travelling        _____

18. grey              _____

19. busses            _____

20. catsup            _____

Name: _____ Date: _____

# Spelling: *Exercise 7 (Plurals)* DICTIONARY

**Directions:** Look up each of these words in a dictionary and write the plural form of the word.

1. deer _____
2. index _____
3. mouse _____
4. fish _____
5. chief _____
6. bass _____
7. trout _____
8. thief _____
9. shelf _____
10. country _____
11. Saturday _____
12. hero _____
13. moose _____
14. roof _____
15. potato _____
16. wolf _____
17. relish _____
18. house _____
19. sundae _____
20. fantasy _____

21. life _____
22. quiz _____
23. crush _____
24. radio _____
25. prefix _____
26. watch _____
27. strawberry _____
28. eyelash _____
29. victory _____
30. tomato _____
31. tooth _____
32. elf _____
33. studio _____
34. leaf _____
35. peach _____
36. woman _____
37. child _____
38. acorn _____
39. mystery _____
40. spice _____

# Parts of Speech: *Introduction* DICTIONARY

The most common **parts of speech** are noun, verb, adjective, adverb, and preposition.

A **noun** is a word that names a person, place, or thing. In the sentence "My daughter drove her car to school," the words *daughter*, *car*, and *school* are nouns.

A **verb** is a word used to describe an action or condition. In the sentence "My neighbor walked to the grocery store," the word *walked* is a verb.

An **adjective** is a word that describes or modifies a noun or pronoun. In the sentence "The little white dog barked at the gray cat," the words *little*, *white*, and *gray* are adjectives.

An **adverb** is a word that describes or modifies a verb, an adjective, or another adverb. In the sentence, "Two very large vans drove quite slowly down the street," the words *very, quite,* and *slowly* are adverbs.

A **preposition** is a word that shows the relation between another word and a noun or pronoun. In the sentence "The teacher in my class is going on the field trip with us," the words *in, on,* and *with* are prepositions.

Some common abbreviations used in dictionaries for parts of speech are listed below.

adj.    adjective
adv.    adverb
conj.   conjunction
interj. interjection
n.      noun
prep.   preposition
pron.   pronoun
v.      verb

Name: _____ Date: _____

# Parts of Speech: *Exercise 1* DICTIONARY

**Directions:** In a dictionary "n" means noun, "v" means verb, "adj" means adjective, "adv" means adverb, and "prep" means preposition. Identify the correct part of speech for each bold-faced word. Use a dictionary if you need help.

1. Our team hopes to **produce** the winning project. _____

2. Did you light the **match** before you started the fire? _____

3. Don't **stray** too far from home; it's almost dinner time. _____

4. I **might** have to stay home tonight instead of going to the movie. _____

5. Laura went **over** the fence to get the baseball. _____

6. The box of cookies is **empty**. _____

7. If you study, it will lessen your chances of getting a poor **grade**. _____

8. The lemon was bright **yellow**. _____

9. The **wax** on the candles started to melt in the heat. _____

10. We took a tour **through** the cave. _____

11. Did you know you need to **prime** a water pump? _____

12. First **chill** the glasses to keep the lemonade cold. _____

13. The chess competition ended in a **draw**. _____

14. I know an **escape** route if we need it. _____

15. Let's **watch** for the freight train. _____

16. Do you have **change** for a five dollar bill? _____

17. Can you **match** the words with their definitions? _____

18. The moon will **wax** from new to full. _____

19. Is 29 a **prime** number? _____

20. **Empty** the trash cans before you leave. _____

58

Name: _____ Date: _____

# Parts of Speech: *Exercise 2* DICTIONARY

**Directions:** In a dictionary "n" means noun, "v" means verb, "adj" means adjective, "adv" means adverb, and "prep" means preposition. Identify the correct part of speech for each bold-faced word. Use a dictionary if you need help.

1. John jogged **slowly** down the street. _____

2. Michelle took a **drink** of the lemonade. _____

3. Ashley **hates** to go swimming early in the morning. _____

4. I took one of the **chocolate** cookies. _____

5. Have you ever gone to a **produce** stand to shop? _____

6. Dad likes to watch the **baseball** games on television. _____

7. There were loud **shouts** from the football stands. _____

8. Could you stand **behind** the desk? _____

9. Mr. Osborne **grows** pink roses. _____

10. I need a **copy** of the paper by tomorrow. _____

11. I will **plant** the vegetable seeds today. _____

12. **Quickly** open your books. _____

13. Who will **copy** the notes from the board? _____

14. Did I see you **with** them yesterday at the park? _____

15. Look at that **beautiful** sunset. _____

16. The dog will **drink** the water after it eats. _____

17. Have you seen the pepper **plant** in my garden? _____

18. The crowd **shouts** every time a run is scored. _____

19. Is there a gas station **near** your house? _____

20. The old horse is **very** slow. _____

Name: _____ Date: _____

# Parts of Speech: *Exercise 3* DICTIONARY

**Directions:** Using a dictionary, look up two definitions for each of these words. Write the two definitions on the lines. After each definition, write the part of speech the word represents.

1. catch _____

   _____

2. plant _____

   _____

3. copy _____

   _____

4. holiday _____

   _____

5. flower _____

   _____

6. match _____

   _____

7. slick _____

   _____

8. wax _____

   _____

9. yellow _____

   _____

10. tag _____

    _____

Name: _____ Date: _____

# Parts of Speech: *Exercise 4* DICTIONARY

**Directions:** Using a dictionary, look up two definitions for each of these words. Write the two definitions on the lines. After each definition, write the part of speech the word represents.

1. register _____

   _____

2. bolt _____

   _____

3. chime _____

   _____

4. Chinese _____

   _____

5. range _____

   _____

6. produce _____

   _____

7. farrow _____

   _____

8. drill _____

   _____

9. American _____

   _____

10. wonder _____

   _____

# Synonyms: *Introduction* DICTIONARY

A **synonym** is a word that has the same or almost the same meaning as another word. Synonyms help us make our writing clearer and more interesting. Some words are so close in meaning that they can replace each other in a sentence. For example, the synonyms *mistake* and *error* can be used in the same sentence: "The student made a *mistake (error)* on his homework."

Some synonyms, such as *make, form, and manufacture* are not close enough in meaning to be used for one another. You must understand the meanings of these synonyms before they can be used properly in a sentence.

Name: _____ Date: _____

# Synonyms: *Exercise 1* DICTIONARY

**Directions:** One-word definitions are synonyms for a dictionary entry. Synonyms are also listed at the end of a dictionary entry. Circle the synonym for each of the following words.

| | | | | |
|---|---|---|---|---|
| 1. | glance | a. look | b. under | c. create |
| 2. | darken | a. wilted | b. dim | c. listen |
| 3. | fearless | a. fearful | b. careful | c. bold |
| 4. | remote | a. taken | b. distant | c. unhappy |
| 5. | desolate | a. deceive | b. winning | c. solitary |
| 6. | transparent | a. clear | b. carry | c. move |
| 7. | inflate | a. decide | b. expand | c. part |
| 8. | trustworthy | a. honest | b. happy | c. unusual |
| 9. | lengthy | a. leggy | b. long | c. talkative |
| 10. | irritate | a. please | b. input | c. provoke |
| 11. | exterminate | a. destroy | b. build | c. consume |
| 12. | level | a. flat | b. rolling | c. curve |
| 13. | boast | a. brag | b. yell | c. cook |
| 14. | converse | a. run | b. animate | c. talk |
| 15. | admonish | a. warn | b. attempt | c. calculate |

Name: _____ Date: _____

# Synonyms: *Exercise 2* DICTIONARY

**Directions:** One-word definitions are synonyms for a dictionary entry. Synonyms are also listed at the end of a dictionary entry. Circle the synonyms for each of the following words. There may be more than one synonym for each word

| | | | | | |
|---|---|---|---|---|---|
| 1. | final | a. last | b. end | c. latest | d. first |
| 2. | pitch | a. wish | b. toss | c. throw | d. catch |
| 3. | litter | a. letter | b. trash | c. refuse | d. window |
| 4. | exit | a. door | b. enter | c. leave | d. stay |
| 5. | moist | a. humid | b. damp | c. dry | d. wet |
| 6. | buy | a. sell | b. soap | c. purchase | d. obtain |
| 7. | anger | a. rage | b. happiness | c. irritation | d. want |
| 8. | hurry | a. dash | b. rush | c. wait | d. still |
| 9. | under | a. upper | b. beneath | c. below | d. bellow |
| 10. | truth | a. table | b. honesty | c. lie | d. fact |
| 11. | remain | a. stay | b. wait | c. linger | d. leave |
| 12. | neat | a. tidy | b. messy | c. open | d. organized |
| 13. | inquire | a. tell | b. ask | c. request | d. require |
| 14. | ill | a. said | b. sick | c. unwell | d. welcome |
| 15. | mistake | a. error | b. even | c. open | d. fault |

Name: _____ Date: _____

# Synonyms: *Exercise 3* DICTIONARY

**Directions:** Using a dictionary, write a synonym for each of the following words. Then write a sentence using the original word.

1. outcome _____

_____

2. wealthy _____

_____

3. center _____

_____

4. mysterious _____

_____

5. gather _____

_____

6. explosion _____

_____

7. weary _____

_____

8. surprise _____

_____

9. forever _____

_____

10. pledge _____

_____

Name: _____ Date: _____

# Synonyms: *Exercise 4* DICTIONARY

**Directions:** Using a dictionary, write a synonym for each of the following words. Then write a sentence using the original word.

1. cry       _____

_____

2. plain       _____

_____

3. inflate       _____

_____

4. disappear       _____

_____

5. reply       _____

_____

6. frown       _____

_____

7. agree       _____

_____

8. locate       _____

_____

9. comical       _____

_____

10. decline       _____

_____

Name: _____ Date: _____

# Synonyms: *Exercise 5* DICTIONARY

**Directions:** Using a dictionary, write a synonym for each of the following words. Then write a sentence using the original word.

1. ostentatious _____

_____

2. encroach _____

_____

3. inherent _____

_____

4. benefit _____

_____

5. precise _____

_____

6. redundant _____

_____

7. vogue _____

_____

8. meticulous _____

_____

9. agitate _____

_____

10. sulky _____

_____

Name: _____ Date: _____

# Synonyms: *Exercise 6* DICTIONARY

**Directions:** For each clue below, write a synonym in the crossword puzzle.

|   | **ACROSS** |   |   |   | **DOWN** |   |
|---|---|---|---|---|---|---|
| 2. | join | 14. | smell | 1. | scared | 11. | forever |
| 6. | trash | 16. | amaze | 3. | seize | 12. | task |
| 7. | middle | 18. | tidy | 4. | prank | 13. | repair |
| 8. | find | 19. | rich | 5. | touch | 15. | stay |
| 10. | simple | 20. | gentle | 9. | awkward | 17. | ache |

68

# Usage: *Introduction*  DICTIONARY

Dictionaries explain how a word is used, and many times there are several meanings to a single word. Besides the common meaning of a word, there are other meanings that are marked with **usage labels.**

Some examples of usage labels are **[slang]** for slang use, **[informal]** for informal speech, **[dial]** for dialect of a country or region, **[obs]** for obsolete or no longer used, and **[archaic]** for rarely used today.

**Slang -** An informal word used in everyday conversation. An example of slang is the word *doll*, meaning "pleasant or helpful"; *to get dolled up*, meaning "to dress smartly."

**Informal -** A casual word used in place of the more proper word. An example of an informal word is *gal*, meaning "girl."

**Dialect -** A word used regularly only in some areas of the United States. An example of dialect is the word *haunt*, which in some areas of the United States is used as a noun meaning "ghost or spirit."

**Obsolete -** A word definition that is no longer used today, but is still used in earlier writings. An example of an obsolete definition of the word *cog* is "a deception or trick."

**Archaic -** A defintion rarely used today except in certain contexts, such as in church rituals; an archaic definition mainly occurs in earlier writings. An example of an archaic word is *methinks*, meaning "It seems to me."

Name: _____ Date: _____

# Usage: *Exercise 1*   DICTIONARY

**Directions:** Look up the following words in a dictionary and write the correct usage label on the line next to the word. The usage labels are *slang, informal, dialect, obsolete,* and *archaic.*

1.  corny _____

2.  hoodwink _____

3.  pone _____

4.  critter _____

5.  afeared _____

6.  lam _____

7.  chivvy _____

8.  petrol _____

9.  flub _____

10. cheapie _____

**Directions:** Find five words in the dictionary with a usage label. Write the usage label and a definition of each word on the lines below.

1.  _____

2.  _____

3.  _____

4.  _____

5.  _____

Name: _____ Date: _____

# Usage: *Exercise 2* DICTIONARY

**Directions:** Choose the correct word for each sentence. Write the dictionary spelling in the blank. Use a dictionary if you need help. Each word will be used in two different sentences.

| refuse | tear | do | dove |
|--------|------|-----|------|
| bass | close | minute | |

1. We _____ into the swimming pool from the high diving board.

2. There was a _____ spot on Jane's blouse that only she could see.

3. The basket of papers is too _____ to the fire.

4. Please put the _____ in the trash container.

5. You must _____ the door to keep the bugs out of the house.

6. Did you _____ your jacket on the nail?

7. My dad played the _____ drum in the band when he was in school.

8. I _____ to answer any more questions.

9. Is _____ the second note on the musical scale?

10. I saw a white _____ come out of the magician's hat.

11. The _____ Waltz is played in sixty seconds.

12. The girl shed one small _____ when she was sad.

13. That pond only has _____ and sunfish in it.

14. What are you going to _____ now that school is out?

Name: _____ Date: _____

## Usage: *Exercise 3*    DICTIONARY

**Directions:** Choose the correct word for each sentence. Write the dictionary spelling in the blank. Use a dictionary if you need help. Each word will be used in two different sentences.

| | | | |
|---|---|---|---|
| lead | live | wind | bow |
| polish | present | does | |

1. You need to _____ your shoes before you go to the party.

2. Mom, are we having _____ sausage for dinner tonight?

3. There were six _____ standing with their fawns.

4. The weatherman said the _____ would be blowing at 60 miles per hour during the storm.

5. Is that the house you _____ in?

6. I haven't bought James a birthday _____ yet.

7. In archery we use a _____ and arrow.

8. What _____ your mother want you to do after school?

9. Matt and Marco will take a _____ after the musical recital.

10. Mrs. Li will _____ the attendance awards today.

11. To make the top work, you have to _____ a string around it.

12. One of the hazards in old buildings is _____ paint.

13. We have _____ goldfish in our garden pond.

14. Mr. White, our oldest veteran, will _____ the July 4th parade.

    72

# Usage: *Exercise 4* DICTIONARY

Name: _____ Date: _____

**Directions:** Choose the correct word for each sentence. Write the dictionary spelling in the blank. Use a dictionary for help. Each word will be used in two different sentences.

| live | sow | moped | invalid |
|------|-----|-------|---------|
| row | excuse | wound | |

1. You collected the wrong data, so your chart will be _____.

2. I am saving my money to buy a _____ to ride on.

3. After the motorcycle accident, John was an _____ in the hospital for a month.

4. The farm has a _____ and six piglets.

5. My dog ran in circles around the tree and _____ her leash around it.

6. Jeremy and Carl argued over the football; they had a big _____.

7. This summer we are going to _____ carrots in our garden.

8. My mom wrote me an _____ for being absent from school.

9. When her friends didn't call, my sister _____ around the house.

10. On a summer day, it's fun to _____ the boat around the lake.

11. During the Civil War, a soldier often died from his _____.

12. Will you please _____ my brother's bad manners?

13. I _____ at the corner of Maine Street and Vermont Street.

14. On Saturday, you can watch that rock band's concert _____ on television.

73

Name: _____     Date: _____

# Usage: *Exercise 5*     DICTIONARY

**Directions:** For each of the following sentences, use context clues to find the correct definition in the dictionary for the bold-faced word. Write the definition on the line below each sentence.

1. Sarah made a **rough** drawing of the classroom.

   _____

2. When I asked John for the money he owed me, he gave me a **blank** look.

   _____

3. Peter **illuminated** the backyard with the flip of a switch.

   _____

4. You have to plant flower seeds to a **uniform** depth.

   _____

5. I think the **catch** on my watchband is broken.

   _____

6. The Middle East is sometimes called the **cradle** of civilization.

   _____

7. We have to do **exercise** numbers six and seven in our math books.

   _____

8. In the castle, the maid **draws** the queen's bath.

   _____

9. Some mornings I am **pressed** for time because I wake up late.

   _____

10. My brothers sometimes **try** my patience.

   _____

# Run-on Entries: *Introduction*

At the end of a dictionary entry, there are often prefixes or suffixes added to the end of the word that give it a different meaning. These are called **run-on entries**. There usually isn't a definition for the run-on entries, but the part of speech is listed, such as *noun or adverb*. For example, after the definitions for the word *great*, you would see *-ly, adv.,* and *-ness, n.* These words are related to the word *great*, but have a different meaning.

Name: _____ Date: _____

# Run-on Entries: *Exercise 1* DICTIONARY

**Example:** *Happy* is the entry word and is an adjective. At the end of the definition, *-happiness n.* and *-happily adv.* are listed.

**Directions:** Using a dictionary, write a run-on entry for each of the following words.

1. bad _____

2. smooth _____

3. raspy _____

4. fluff _____

5. cerebral _____

6. rough _____

7. federal _____

8. feeling _____

9. redo _____

10. transition _____

11. fair _____

12. thin _____

13. wish _____

14. wire _____

15. social _____

Happy   happiness   happily

Name: _____   Date: _____

# Run-on Entries: *Exercise 2* DICTIONARY

**Directions:** Using a dictionary, find the run-on entry for each of these words and write the part of speech for the run-on entry. Then write a definition for the run-on entry.

1.  foolish          _____        _____

    _____

2.  rapid            _____        _____

    _____

3.  careful          _____        _____

    _____

4.  inscribe         _____        _____

    _____

5.  cold             _____        _____

    _____

6.  water            _____        _____

    _____

7.  connect          _____        _____

    _____

8.  reform           _____        _____

    _____

9.  lonesome         _____        _____

    _____

10. pad              _____        _____

    _____

Name: _____ Date: _____

# Dictionary Skills Practice: *Exercise 1*

**Directions:** Using a dictionary, look up each of the following words and write the answers in the correct column next to each word. Then pronounce each word to yourself.

| Word | Guide Words | Dictionary Spelling | Written in Syllables |
|------|-------------|---------------------|----------------------|
| 1. excite | _____ | _____ | _____ |
| 2. individual | _____ | _____ | _____ |
| 3. cabinet | _____ | _____ | _____ |
| 4. dozen | _____ | _____ | _____ |
| 5. celebrate | _____ | _____ | _____ |
| 6. perhaps | _____ | _____ | _____ |
| 7. weigh | _____ | _____ | _____ |
| 8. diversity | _____ | _____ | _____ |
| 9. coax | _____ | _____ | _____ |
| 10. sure | _____ | _____ | _____ |
| 11. reform | _____ | _____ | _____ |
| 12. negative | _____ | _____ | _____ |
| 13. business | _____ | _____ | _____ |
| 14. negotiate | _____ | _____ | _____ |
| 15. pensive | _____ | _____ | _____ |

Name: _____ Date: _____

# Dictionary Skills Practice: *Exercise 2*

**Directions:** Using a dictionary, look up each of the following words and write the answers in the correct column next to each word. Then pronounce each word to yourself.

| Word | Guide Words | Dictionary Spelling | Written in Syllables |
|------|-------------|---------------------|----------------------|
| 1. opportunity | | | |
| 2. decimal | | | |
| 3. navigate | | | |
| 4. cradled | | | |
| 5. ambition | | | |
| 6. wailing | | | |
| 7. fable | | | |
| 8. noble | | | |
| 9. fair | | | |
| 10. mobilize | | | |
| 11. underneath | | | |
| 12. beyond | | | |
| 13. happy | | | |
| 14. stupefy | | | |
| 15. dread | | | |

Name: _____  Date: _____

# Dictionary Skills Practice: *Exercise 3* DICTIONARY

**Directions:** Using a dictionary, look up each of the following words and write the answers in the correct column next to each word. Then pronounce each word to yourself.

| Word | Guide Words | Dictionary Spelling | Written in Syllables |
|------|-------------|---------------------|----------------------|
| 1. falcon | _____ | _____ | _____ |
| 2. outcome | _____ | _____ | _____ |
| 3. quaint | _____ | _____ | _____ |
| 4. compassion | _____ | _____ | _____ |
| 5. enjoy | _____ | _____ | _____ |
| 6. particular | _____ | _____ | _____ |
| 7. express | _____ | _____ | _____ |
| 8. traveler | _____ | _____ | _____ |
| 9. boisterous | _____ | _____ | _____ |
| 10. driven | _____ | _____ | _____ |
| 11. stretch | _____ | _____ | _____ |
| 12. unbelievable | _____ | _____ | _____ |
| 13. connect | _____ | _____ | _____ |
| 14. special | _____ | _____ | _____ |
| 15. recruit | _____ | _____ | _____ |

DICTIONARY

Name: _____ Date: _____

# Dictionary Skills Practice: *Exercise* 4

**Directions:** Look up these people and places in the dictionary. What is the dictionary definition?

1. Stephen Decatur _____

_____

2. Long Beach _____

_____

3. Sergipe _____

_____

4. Emily Brontë _____

_____

5. FRS _____

_____

6. Charles Willson Peale _____

_____

7. Booker T. Washington _____

_____

8. Robert Burns Woodward _____

_____

9. Kyoto _____

_____

10. Okinawa _____

_____

Name: _____  Date: _____

# Dictionary Skills Practice: *Exercise 5*  DICTIONARY

**Directions:** Look up these people and places in the dictionary. What is the dictionary definition?

1. Oromo _____
_____

2. Ira Gershwin _____
_____

3. Medicine Hat _____
_____

4. Nevis _____
_____

5. American Indian _____
_____

6. Nejd _____
_____

7. Alban Berg _____
_____

8. English Channel _____
_____

9. Hmong _____
_____

10. Samuel Richardson _____
_____

Name: _____ Date: _____

# Dictionary Skills Practice: *Exercise 6*

**Directions:** Using a dictionary, look up each of the bold-faced words and answer the questions that follow.

1. Look up the word **unusual**.

   a. How many syllables are in the word? _____

   b. Write **unusual**, breaking it into syllables. _____

   c. How many definitions does **unusual** have? _____

   d. What is the definition of **unusual**?

   _____

   _____

   e. What part of speech is **unusual**? _____

   f. Use **unusual** in a sentence. _____

   _____

2. Look up the word **beautiful**.

   a. How many syllables are in the word? _____

   b. Write **beautiful**, breaking it into syllables. _____

   c. How many definitions does **beautiful** have? _____

   d. What is the definition of **beautiful**?

   _____

   _____

   e. What part of speech is **beautiful**? _____

   f. Use **beautiful** in a sentence. _____

   _____

Name: _____ Date: _____

# Dictionary Skills Practice: *Exercise 7* DICTIONARY

**Directions:** Using a dictionary, look up each of the bold-faced words and answer the questions that follow.

1. Look up the word **blanket**.

   a. How many syllables are in the word? _____

   b. Write **blanket**, breaking it into syllables. _____

   c. How many definitions does **blanket** have? _____

   d. What is the definition of **blanket**?

   _____

   _____

   e. What part of speech is **blanket**? _____

   f. Use **blanket** in a sentence. _____

   _____

2. Look up the word **considerate**.

   a. How many syllables are in the word? _____

   b. Write **considerate**, breaking it into syllables. _____

   c. How many definitions does **considerate** have? _____

   d. What is the definition of **considerate**?

   _____

   _____

   e. What part of speech is **considerate**? _____

   f. Use **considerate** in a sentence. _____

   _____

Name: _____ Date: _____

# Dictionary Skills Practice: *Exercise 8*

**Directions:** Using a dictionary, look up each of the bold-faced words and answer the questions that follow.

1. Look up the word **liquidate**.

    a. How many syllables are in the word? _____

    b. Write **liquidate**, breaking it into syllables. _____

    c. How many definitions does **liquidate** have? _____

    d. What is the definition of **liquidate**?

    _____

    _____

    e. What part of speech is **liquidate**? _____

    f. Use **liquidate** in a sentence. _____

    _____

2. Look up the word **noxious**.

    a. How many syllables are in the word? _____

    b. Write **noxious**, breaking it into syllables. _____

    c. How many definitions does **noxious** have? _____

    d. What is the definition of **noxious**?

    _____

    _____

    e. What part of speech is **noxious**? _____

    f. Use **noxious** in a sentence. _____

    _____

Name: _____ Date: _____

# Dictionary Skills Practice: *Exercise 9* DICTIONARY

**Directions:** Using a dictionary, look up each of the words your teacher gives you and answer the questions.

1. Look up the word _____.

   a. How many syllables are in the word? _____

   b. Write the word, breaking it into syllables. _____

   c. How many definitions does the word have? _____

   d. What is the definition of the word?

      _____

      _____

   e. What part of speech is the word? _____

   f. Use the word in a sentence. _____

      _____

2. Look up the word _____.

   a. How many syllables are in the word? _____

   b. Write the word, breaking it into syllables. _____

   c. How many definitions does the word have? _____

   d. What is the definition of the word?

      _____

      _____

   e. What part of speech is the word? _____

   f. Use the word in a sentence. _____

      _____

# Answer Keys

## DICTIONARY

### Alphabetical Order: Exercise 1 (p. 2)
1. bitter, north, nut, paint, salute
2. beach, map, mast, noon, ocean
3. auto, breathe, cobra, collision, salon
4. animal, bluff, dive, mummy, numb
5. beauty, gentle, puppy, quick, wave
6. candy, doughnut, pickle, spaghetti, window
7. cartoon, kangaroo, lucky, onion, salt
8. answer, balloon, lucky, many, question
9. donkey, enough, wishful, wonderful, zero
10. eating, hot dog, hungry, juice, sandwich

### Alphabetical Order: Exercise 2 (p. 3)
1. marker, mast, mean, middle, mildew, milk, mince, money, mouse
2. acorn, aisle, ajar, amber, amble, announce, answer, applaud, awake
3. dance, dangle, dapple, deny, dinner, door, drive, drop, dunce
4. paid, path, phone, plea, plow, posture, pride, prize, purse
5. back, bake, bend, bicycle, bitter, blink, bluff, botch, buffalo
6. table, tailor, tank, teller, think, throw, tick, torn, trim
7. name, nape, neon, nine, noon, north, nose, nothing, numb
8. saber, sample, sassy, scissors, settle, simple, sister, skeleton, south
9. came, candle, center, cider, cobra, collision, color, combat, come
10. quaint, quell, quiet, quilt, quince, quit, quite, quiz, quizzical

### Alphabetical Order: Exercise 3 (p. 4)
1. anniversary
2. confuse
3. curtail
4. department store
5. dept.
6. discriminate
7. divine
8. elephant
9. human being
10. marvelous
11. minute
12. money
13. muddle
14. Prof.
15. question
16. Rd.
17. statesman
18. suppose
19. wandering
20. water lily

### Alphabetical Order: Exercise 4 (p. 5)
1. dance
2. danger
3. dear
4. deep
5. defense
6. dent
7. depend
8. deport
9. dept.
10. die
11. dip
12. direct
13. distant
14. donut
15. doughnut
16. Dr.
17. dream
18. drift
19. drove
20. dye

### Alphabetical Order: Exercise 5 (p. 6)
1. hobby
2. hockey
3. hog-tie
4. hold
5. holder
6. Holocaust
7. home
8. home base
9. homing
10. homogenize
11. honor
12. honorary
13. hoot
14. hope
15. hopper
16. horizontal
17. horse
18. host
19. hour
20. how

### Word Placement: Exercise 1 (p. 8)
1. middle
2. last
3. middle
4. first
5. last
6. last
7. middle
8. last
9. last
10. first
11. last
12. last
13. middle
14. middle
15. first

### Word Placement: Exercise 2 (p. 9)
1. middle
2. first
3. last
4. middle
5. last
6. last
7. middle
8. first
9. middle
10. middle
11. middle
12. last
13. first
14. middle
15. last

### Word Placement: Exercise 3 (p. 10)
| | | |
|---|---|---|
| 1. F–P | 2. A–E | 3. F–P |
| 4. Q–Z | 5. F–P | 6. F–P |
| 7. Q–Z | 8. A–E | 9. F–P |
| 10. Q–Z | 11. Q–Z | 12. F–P |
| 13. A–E | 14. F–P | 15. Q–Z |
| 16. Q–Z | 17. F–P | 18. Q–Z |
| 19. Q–Z | 20. Q–Z | 21. F–P |
| 22. Q–Z | 23. A–E | 24. F–P |
| 25. F–P | | |

## Word Placement: Exercise 4 (p. 11)

| | | |
|---|---|---|
| 1. F–P | 2. A–E | 3. F–P |
| 4. Q–Z | 5. A–E | 6. Q–Z |
| 7. F–P | 8. A–E | 9. A–E |
| 10. A–E | 11. F–P | 12. Q–Z |
| 13. A–E | 14. Q–Z | 15. F–P |
| 16. Q–Z | 17. A–E | 18. A–E |
| 19. F–P | 20. F–P | 21. F–P |
| 22. Q–Z | 23. A–E | 24. Q–Z |
| 25. F–P | | |

## Guide Words: Exercise 1 (p. 14)

1. b. arch, c. baboon, e. babble
2. a. elegant, b. danger, e. dive, f. each
3. b. milk, c. lunch, e. march, f. litter
4. a. pal, b. quiet, c. pill, d. pay
5. a. money, b. name, e. multiply, f. never
6. a. talk, c. stole, e. tickle, f. stove
7. a. potato, b. posture, f. potent

## Guide Words: Exercise 2 (p. 15)

1. a. grasp, b. grape, c. graph
2. a. letter, c. level, d. let, e. lettuce
3. b. cupboard, c. curd, d. curb
4. a. ajar, b. Alaska, d. alarm, f. airport
5. a. hibernate, e. hesitate, f. hew
6. b. patient, d. peddle, f. peace
7. b. uncle, c. uncork, d. unchain

## Guide Words: Exercise 3 (p. 16)

1. a. orbit, b. oppose, e. orange, f. orderly
2. b. corn, c. correct, d. corrosive, f. cornice
3. a. shaker, b. shall, d. sharp, f. shame
4. b. menial, c. mercy, d. melting, e. mend
5. a. amend, b. ambush, d. amble
6. a. feel, b. feeder, c. federal, e. feeble
7. a. remark, c. remember, f. relive

## Guide Words: Exercise 4 (p. 17)

1. b. rest, c. resistant, d. responsive, e. resort, h. respect
2. a. gray, c. grave, d. granule, e. gravel, f. graphite, g. gratuity
3. a. calf, b. camera, d. California, g. call
4. a. oversleep, d. overt, e. owlet, f. overstep
5. a. crossfire, c. croak, d. crony, e. critic, f. croquet, h. crop
6. b. already, e. alloy, f. almanac, g. almond
7. b. laugh, c. lava, e. laundry, f. lattice, g. latrine

## Guide Words: Exercise 5 (p. 18)

| | |
|---|---|
| 1. on | 11. after |
| 2. before | 12. on |
| 3. after | 13. after |
| 4. after | 14. before |
| 5. on | 15. after |
| 6. after | 16. after |
| 7. before | 17. on |
| 8. on | 18. before |
| 9. before | 19. after |
| 10. after | 20. on |

## Guide Words: Exercise 6 (p. 19)

| | |
|---|---|
| 1. after | 11. after |
| 2. on | 12. before |
| 3. after | 13. after |
| 4. before | 14. on |
| 5. on | 15. after |
| 6. after | 16. on |
| 7. on | 17. before |
| 8. on | 18. on |
| 9. on | 19. on |
| 10. before | 20. after |

## Meaning: Exercise 1 (p. 21)

| | |
|---|---|
| 1. b | 6. b |
| 2. b | 7. a |
| 3. b | 8. a |
| 4. b | 9. a |
| 5. a | 10. b |

## Meaning: Exercise 2 (p. 22)

| | |
|---|---|
| 1. b | 4. c |
| 2. a | 5. c |
| 3. b | 6. a |

Decoration: Sentences will vary.

## Meaning: Exercise 3 (p. 23)

1. panel: flat piece of wood
2. cover: extend over
3. might: physical strength
4. match: a competition
5. grave: serious
6. relish: chopped vegetables
7. temple: space on either side of the forehead
8. part: role
9. block: hide from view
10. draw: attract

## Meaning: Exercise 4 (p. 24)

1. abroad: to a foreign country
2. leafed: past tense of to turn a page
3. hinges: depends on
4. method: procedure
5. preserve: protected area
6. allowance: money to live on
7. spark: small fire
8. blanket: covering
9. batter: mixture of flour, eggs, etc.
10. trouble: bother

## Meaning: Exercise 5 (p. 25)

Student definitions will vary.

1. cue: word or action to suggest the next line in a play
2. study: a room for reading
3. volume: one book in a set
4. enlist: to arrange for
5. chance: a ticket to try to win a prize
6. dash: a short line

## Meaning: Exercise 6 (p. 26)

Student definitions will vary.

1. right: correct
2. dash: run
3. volume: loudness
4. might: could possibly
5. bow: bent strip of wood with a string attached
6. address: talk to

## Syllables: Exercise 1 (p. 28)

| | |
|---|---|
| 1. po • ta • to | 8. tooth |
| 2. am • ber | 9. shark |
| 3. feath • er | 10. mat • tress |
| 4. meth • od | 11. great |
| 5. ro • dent | 12. desk |
| 6. puz • zle | 13. trou • ble |
| 7. luck • y | 14. ur • gent |

## Syllables: Exercise 2 (p. 29)

1. ex • traor • din • ar • y
2. won • der • ful
3. tel • e • vi • sion
4. suc • ceed • ed

5. for • ev • er
6. sto • len
7. eth • i • cal
8. de • sired
9. af • fec • tion • ate
10. chat
11. pre • serve
12. de • ssert
13. shin • ing
14. quick • ly

**Syllables: Exercise 3 (p. 30)**
1. trust • wor • thy
2. an • tag • o • nist
3. un • be • liev • a • ble
4. mar • vel • ous
5. syn • thet • ic
6. but • ter • scotch
7. blan • ket
8. mem • o • ry
9. some • times
10. me • thod • i • cal
11. ad • di • tion • al
12. par • tic • u • lar • ly
13. com • plete
14. me • trop • o • lis

**Syllables: Exercise 4 (p. 31)**
1. un • hap • py     2. pic • ture
3. friend • ly       4. look • out
5. dam • age        6. key • board
7. de • cide        8. wish • ful
9. par • ty         10. rid • dle
11. dis • tant      12. ear • ly
13. fend • er       14. pick • le
15. pup • py        16. gre • nade
17. siz • zle       18. mar • vel
19. him • self      20. em • ploy

**Syllables: Exercise 5 (p. 32)**
| | |
|---|---|
| 1. 4 | 2. 2 |
| 3. 2 | 4. 3 |
| 5. 4 | 6. 2 |
| 7. 2 | 8. 1 |
| 9. 2 | 10. 1 |
| 11. 4 | 12. 1 |
| 13. 3 | 14. 1 |
| 15. 2 | 16. 3 |
| 17. 4 | 18. 5 |
| 19. 2 | 20. 3 |
| 21. 2 | 22. 3 |
| 23. 4 | 24. 2 |
| 25. 4 | 26. 3 |
| 27. 5 | 28. 4 |
| 29. 3 | 30. 2 |

**Pronunciation: Exercise 4 (p. 37)**
1. ē nuf′       2. wāt
3. bōld         4. ob jekt′, əb jekt′
5. kan′ dl      6. stäk
7. nev′ ər      8. ī dē′ ə
9. kəm plēt′ lē  10. ruf
11. kwik′ lē    12. mel′ ō
13. rān         14. kōp

**Pronunciation: Exercise 5 (p. 38)**
1. ten′ shən    2. dē fens′
3. sēz          4. rō′ lər
5. pēs′ fəl     6. əb zûrv′
7. fēr′ fəl     8. sub′ sti tōōt′
9. sek′ ənd    10. nā′ shən
11. pov′ ər tē  12. i myōōn′
13. kə lek′ shən  14. slip′ ə rē

**Pronunciation: Exercise 6 (p. 39)**
1. pecan        2. carnival
3. fear         4. acre
5. nose         6. catch
7. spat         8. roller
9. deaf         10. television
11. speak       12. telephone
13. beach       14. horror
15. overlay

**Pronunciation: Exercise 7 (p. 40)**

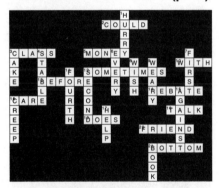

**Pronunciation: Exercise 8 (p. 41)**

**Prefixes and Suffixes: Exercise 1 (p. 43)**
There may be more than one possibility for some words.
1. **re**living: live again
2. **un**hurt: not hurt
3. **dis**agree: not agree
4. **un**do: reverse the doing of
5. **pre**arrange: arrange before
6. **non**working: not working
7. **non**flammable: not flammable
8. **pre**soak: soak before
9. **un**lawful: not lawful
10. **re**turn: turn again

**Prefixes and Suffixes: Exercise 2 (p. 44)**
There may be more than one possibility for some words.
1. **non**stick: without sticking
2. **un**usual: not usual
3. **dis**appear: to cease to appear
4. **un**cooperative: not cooperative
5. **non**refundable: not refundable
6. **pre**packaged: packaged before
7. **pre**dawn: before dawn
8. **re**view: view again
9. **un**happy: not happy
10. **non**stop: without a stop

**Prefixes and Suffixes: Exercise 3 (p. 45)**
1. ful; beauty: pleasing to the eye
2. ous; danger: harm
3. able; break: smash
4. ing; move: change position
5. ful; pity: sympathy
6. less; thought: mental activity
7. able; drink: to take liquid into the body
8. est; strange: odd
9. er; carry: to haul or pack
10. ible; reverse: to go back

**Prefixes and Suffixes: Exercise 4 (p. 46)**
1. ness; happy: joyful
2. ful; wonder: awe
3. est; lazy: idle
4. able; consume: to use
5. ish; fool: silly person
6. some; tire: to grow weary
7. ion; celebrate: to participate in a party or holiday

8. ment; employ: to hire
9. ence; persist: to continue
10. ment; content: satisfied

## Prefixes and Suffixes: Exercise 5 (p. 47)

| | Prefix | Suffix | Base |
|---|---|---|---|
| 1. | | able | vary |
| 2. | | ing | follow |
| 3. | dis | ed | interest |
| 4. | | ible | sense |
| 5. | un | ly | happy |
| 6. | | ible | convert |
| 7. | dis | ed | joint |
| 8. | re | ed | order |
| 9. | non | | fiction |
| 10. | | ness | happy |
| 11. | pre | ed | arrange |
| 12. | un | able | speak |
| 13. | non | ous | poison |
| 14. | mis | ed | inform |
| 15. | re | ion | construct |
| 16. | | ful | right |
| 17. | mono | | tone |
| 18. | hydro | | therapy |
| 19. | en | ment | tangle |
| 20. | un | ed | complicate |

## Prefixes and Suffixes: Exercise 6 (p. 48)

| | Prefix | Suffix | Base |
|---|---|---|---|
| 1. | | less | defense |
| 2. | | er | run |
| 3. | | able | excuse |
| 4. | pre | | school |
| 5. | | ful | wonder |
| 6. | | li, ness | friend |
| 7. | non | | dairy |
| 8. | un | able | forget |
| 9. | re | able | use |
| 10. | mis | | cast |
| 11. | un | able | answer |
| 12. | | ing, ness | will |
| 13. | | able | manage |
| 14. | | ed | succeed |
| 15. | dis | ed | enchant |
| 16. | super | | human |
| 17. | pre | ed | destine |
| 18. | ex | | change |
| 19. | bi | ly | month |
| 20. | quadra | ic | phone |

## Spelling: Exercise 1 (p. 50)

| | | | |
|---|---|---|---|
| 1. correct | | 2. martyr |
| 3. correct | | 4. license |
| 5. answer | | 6. correct |
| 7. calendar | | 8. correct |
| 9. spaghetti | | 10. remember |
| 11. accurate | | 12. correct |
| 13. freight | | 14. correct |
| 15. forty | | |

## Spelling: Exercise 2 (p. 51)

| | |
|---|---|
| 1. correct | 2. sugar |
| 3. bouquet | 4. correct |
| 5. often | 6. difficulties |
| 7. occurrence | 8. correct |
| 9. surprised | 10. correct |
| 11. policy | 12. correct |
| 13. correct | 14. guarantee |
| 15. vacuum | |

## Spelling: Exercise 3 (p. 52)

| | |
|---|---|
| 1. reef | 2. correct |
| 3. correct | 4. nocturnal |
| 5. correct | 6. floral |
| 7. writing | 8. correct |
| 9. correct | 10. approval |
| 11. burial | 12. correct |
| 13. assignment | 14. correct |
| 15. truly | |

## Spelling: Exercise 4 (p. 53)

| | |
|---|---|
| 1. develop | 2. worrisome |
| 3. mystery | 4. unusual |
| 5. opportunity | 6. because |
| 7. similar | 8. escape |
| 9. operator | 10. adjourn |
| 11. alert | 12. neighbor |
| 13. people | 14. autumn |
| 15. tolerate | 16. argument |
| 17. loveliness | 18. meanness |
| 19. advantageous | 20. occurred |
| 21. beautiful | 22. joking |
| 23. believe | 24. permitting |
| 25. thief | 26. begged |
| 27. tortoise | 28. receipt |
| 29. privilege | 30. circular |

## Spelling: Exercise 5 (p. 54)

| | |
|---|---|
| 1. happened | 2. crawl |
| 3. alert | 4. special |
| 5. friend | 6. illogical |
| 7. column | 8. anxious |
| 9. yield | 10. elementary |
| 11. controlled | 12. physician |
| 13. familiar | 14. unnecessary |
| 15. conscience | 16. venom |
| 17. nuclear | 18. receive |
| 19. moose | 20. different |
| 21. compose | 22. astronaut |
| 23. monkeys | 24. expect |
| 25. scratch | 26. landscape |
| 27. wrecked | 28. geese |
| 29. timing | 30. valleys |

## Spelling: Exercise 6 (p. 55)

| | |
|---|---|
| 1. cancelled | 2. cantaloup |
| 3. esthetic | 4. judgment* |
| 5. monologue* | 6. likable* |
| 7. gauge* | 8. hearken* |
| 9. brooch* | 10. abridgment* |
| 11. donut | 12. dialogue* |
| 13. coconut* | 14. travelogue* |
| 15. ricksha | 16. labour |
| 17. traveling* | 18. gray* |
| 19. buses* | 20. ketchup* |

## Spelling: Exercise 7 (p. 56)

1. deer
2. indexes or indices
3. mice
4. fish or fishes (plural species)
5. chiefs
6. basses or bass (fish)
7. trout
8. thieves
9. shelves
10. countries
11. Saturdays
12. heroes
13. moose
14. roofs
15. potatoes
16. wolves
17. relishes
18. houses
19. sundaes
20. fantasies
21. lives
22. quizzes
23. crushes
24. radios
25. prefixes
26. watches
27. strawberries
28. eyelashes
29. victories
30. tomatoes
31. teeth

32. elves
33. studios
34. leaves
35. peaches
36. women
37. children
38. acorns
39. mysteries
40. spices

## Parts of Speech: Exercise 1 (p. 58)

| | |
|---|---|
| 1. v | 11. v |
| 2. n | 12. v |
| 3. v | 13. n |
| 4. v | 14. adj |
| 5. prep | 15. v |
| 6. adj | 16. n |
| 7. n | 17. v |
| 8. adj | 18. v |
| 9. n | 19. adj |
| 10. prep | 20. v |

## Parts of Speech: Exercise 2 (p. 59)

| | |
|---|---|
| 1. adv | 11. v |
| 2. n | 12. adv |
| 3. v | 13. v |
| 4. adj | 14. prep |
| 5. adj | 15. adj |
| 6. adj | 16. v |
| 7. n | 17. n |
| 8. prep | 18. v |
| 9. v | 19. prep |
| 10. n | 20. adv |

## Synonyms: Exercise 1 (p. 63)

| | |
|---|---|
| 1. a. look | 9. b. long |
| 2. b. dim | 10. c. provoke |
| 3. c. bold | 11. a. destroy |
| 4. b. distant | 12. a. flat |
| 5. c. solitary | 13. a. brag |
| 6. a. clear | 14. c. talk |
| 7. b. expand | 15. a. warn |
| 8. a. honest | |

## Synonyms: Exercise 2 (p. 64)

1. a. last, b. end, c. latest
2. b. toss, c. throw
3. b. trash, c. refuse
4. a. door, c. leave
5. a. humid, b. damp, d. wet
6. c. purchase, d. obtain
7. a. rage, c. irritation
8. a. dash, b. rush
9. b. beneath, c. below

10. b. honesty, d. fact
11. a. stay, b. wait c. linger
12. a. tidy, d. organized
13. b. ask, c. request
14. b. sick, c. unwell
15. a. error, d. fault

## Synonyms: Exercise 6 (p. 68)

## Usage: Exercise 1 (p. 70)

| | |
|---|---|
| 1. slang | 6. slang |
| 2. archaic | 7. dial |
| 3. dial | 8. dial |
| 4. dial | 9. slang |
| 5. dial | 10. slang |

Remaining words will vary.

## Usage: Exercise 2 (p. 71)

| | |
|---|---|
| 1. dōv | 8. ri fyo͞oz′ |
| 2. mi no͞ot′ | 9. do͞ |
| 3. klōs | 10. duv |
| 4. ref′ yo͞os | 11. min′ it |
| 5. klōz | 12. tîr |
| 6. târ | 13. bas |
| 7. bās | 14. do͞o |

## Usage: Exercise 3 (p. 72)

| | |
|---|---|
| 1. pol′ ish | 8. duz |
| 2. pō′ lish | 9. bou |
| 3. dōz | 10. pri zent′ |
| 4. wind | 11. wīnd |
| 5. liv | 12. led |
| 6. prez′ ənt | 13. līv |
| 7. bō | 14. lēd |

## Usage: Exercise 4 (p. 73)

| | |
|---|---|
| 1. in val′ id | 8. ik skyo͞os′ |
| 2. mō′ ped | 9. mōpd |
| 3. in′ və lid | 10. rō |
| 4. sou | 11. wo͞ond |
| 5. wound | 12. ik skyo͞oz′ |
| 6. rou | 13. liv |
| 7. sō | 14. līv |

## Usage: Exercise 5 (p. 74)

1. rough: crude
2. blank: without expression
3. illuminated: shined light on
4. uniform: even, equal
5. catch: hook, clasp
6. cradle: beginning, birthplace
7. exercise: activity, problem
8. draws: to run water
9. pressed: hurried
10. try: to test

## Dictionary Skills Practice: Exercise 1 (p. 78)

Guide words will vary.

| | |
|---|---|
| 1. ik sīt′ | ex • cite |
| 2. in′ də vij′ o͞o əl | in • di • vid • u • al |
| 3. kab′ ə net | cab • i • net |
| 4. duz′ ən | doz • en |
| 5. sel′ ə brāt′ | cel • e • brate |
| 6. pər haps′ | per • haps |
| 7. wā | weigh |
| 8. di vûr′ si tē | di • ver • si • ty |
| 9. kōks | coax |
| 10. sho͞or, shûr | sure |
| 11. rē′ fôrm′, ri fôrm′ | re • form |
| 12. neg′ ə tiv | neg • a • tive |
| 13. biz′ nis | busi • ness |
| 14. ni gō′ shē āt′ | ne • go • ti • ate |
| 15. pen′ siv | pen • sive |

## Dictionary Skills Practice: Exercise 2 (p. 79)

Guide words will vary.

| | |
|---|---|
| 1. op′ ər to͞o′ ni tē | op•por•tu•ni•ty |
| 2. des′ ə məl | dec • i • mal |
| 3. nav′ i gāt′ | nav • i • gate |
| 4. krād′ 'ld | cra • dled |
| 5. am bish′ ən | am • bi • tion |
| 6. wāl′ ing | wail • ing |
| 7. fā′ bəl | fa • ble |
| 8. nō′ bəl | no • ble |
| 9. fâr | fair |
| 10. mō′ bə līz′ | mo • bi • lize |
| 11. un′ dər nēth′ | un • der • neath |
| 12. bē ond′ | be • yond |
| 13. hap′ ē | hap • py |
| 14. sto͞o′ pə fī′ | stu • pe • fy |
| 15. dred | dread |

**Dictionary Skills Practice:**
**Exercise 3 (p. 80)**
Guide words will vary.
1. fȯl′ kən, fal′ kən    fal • con
2. out′ kum′         out • come
3. kwānt            quaint
4. kəm pash′ ən   com • pas • sion
5. en joi′           en • joy
6. pər tik′ yə lər   par • tic • u • lar
7. ik spres′        ex • press
8. trav′ əl ər      trav • el • er
9. boi′ stər əs     bois • ter • ous
10. driv′ ən       driv • en
11. strech          stretch
12. un′ bi lē′ və bəl
     un • be • liev • a • ble
13. kə nekt′        con • nect
14. spesh′ əl       spe • cial
15. ri kro͞ot′        re • cruit

**Dictionary Skills Practice:**
**Exercise 4 (p. 81)**
1. a naval officer
2. a city in California
3. a state in Brazil
4. an English novelist
5. Fellow of the Royal Society
6. a painter
7. an African-American reformer and educator
8. a chemist
9. a city in Japan
10. an island owned by Japan

**Dictionary Skills Practice:**
**Exercise 5 (p. 82)**
1. an African person
2. a composer
3. a city in Canada
4. an island in the eastern Caribbean Sea
5. an indigenous person in North or South America
6. Saudi Arabia
7. a composer
8. body of water between England and France
9. a group from China
10. a novelist

**Dictionary Skills Practice:**
**Exercise 6 (p. 83)**
Answers c., d., and f. will vary.
1. a. 4
   b. un • u • su • al
   e. adj
2. a. 3
   b. beau • ti • ful
   e. adj

**Dictionary Skills Practice:**
**Exercise 7 (p. 84)**
Answers c., d., and f. will vary.
1. a. 2
   b. blan • ket
   e. n or v
2. a. 4
   b. con • sid • er • ate
   e. adj

**Dictionary Skills Practice:**
**Exercise 8 (p. 85)**
Answers c., d., and f. will vary.
1. a. 3
   b. liq • ui • date
   e. v
2. a. 2
   b. nox • ious
   e. adj